THE

Art

OF

Pressed

Flowers

THE

Art

OF

Pressed

Flowers

Mary
Lawrence

Running Press

2002 Salamander Ltd
Published by Salamander Books Limited
8 Blenheim Court, Brewery Road
London N7 9NY, United Kingdom

©Salamander Books Ltd
A member of the Chrysalis Group plc

This edition published in the United States in 2002
by Running Press Book Publishers

9 8 7 6 5 4 3 2 1
Digit on the right indicates the number of this printing

Library of Congress Cataloging-in-Publication Number
2001094430

ISBN 0-7624-1229-1

Credits
Project managed by: Stella Caldwell
Editors: Jilly Glassborow, Sara Phillips, Coral Walker
Designer: Cara Hamilton
Photographer: Steve Tanner
Production: Phillip Chamberlain
Printed and bound in China

This kit may be ordered by mail from the publisher.
Please include $2.50 for postage and handling.
But try your bookstore first!

Running Press Book Publishers
125 South Twenty-second Street,
Philadelphia, Pennsylvania 19103-4399

Visit us on the web!
www.runningpress.com

CONTENTS

INTRODUCTION

Making pressed flower arrangements is such a delightful hobby because it involves so much more than simply creating the designs – much of the pleasure comes from the hours spent in the garden cultivating the plants, the long lazy walks in the country gathering wild flowers, and the preparation and pressing of the flowers and foliage at home. And when it comes to making the designs themselves, there is the pleasure of planning them – deciding which flowers to use, what shapes to make, what color schemes to create.

This colorful book will see you through all the various stages from gathering the flowers to the finished design. There is information on growing and gathering plants, which flowers are most suitable for pressing, and how to press the flowers, create a greeting card or mount and frame a design. There is also plenty of advice on the various techniques you will need to employ when creating your designs. And finally, there are the designs themselves – over 35 beautiful creations from which to choose, ranging from easy-to-make Christmas and birthday cards, through more complex pictures to some delightful novelty ideas that make use of all kinds of items around the home.

In most cases plants have been given their common names, except in those instances where the Latin name is more often used. But, as common names can vary so much, the scientific names of plants have also been given at the back of the book.

Pressed Flowers

The way nature has fashioned flowers gives us great but short-lived pleasure and delight; capture this delight by pressing flowers and you will have the perfect medium for creating pictures of lasting beauty. To enjoy collecting and pressing you do not have to act like a botanist seeking specimens, but your enjoyment of the countryside will increase as you start to look more closely at what is growing there. Examine the structure of each flower you find and learn to appreciate, for instance, the beauty in a single floret of wild chervil or the exquisite detail of the veining of a rose leaf. Try also to learn the plants' names. You will soon discover which plants are most suitable for pressing and when best to pick them.

Gathering Wild Flowers

There is an amazing variety of wild flowers, many of which you may never have previously noticed, and if you gather sparingly from the countryside, you will not harm the plant's future growth. However, do pay attention to the official list of protected plants that you may not pick. Don't break off stems or pull up roots, but cleanly cut the parts you require with scissors. If you place the cut flowers in an opaque plastic carrier bag, blow it up like a balloon and seal it and they will keep well for a few hours. Don't forget also to gather leaves, tendrils, stems, grasses and seedheads. Among the best leaves are those of carrot, meadowsweet, wild chervil, rose, wild strawberry, silverweed, vetch, cherry, maple, sumach and virginia creeper.

Flowers To Grow Or Buy

Annuals, perennials, shrubs and trees all provide material for pressing and even if you only have a window box, you can sow alyssum, candytuft, forget-me-not, lobelia and English primrose. Succulent and fleshy flowers contain too much moisture to press successfully. Multi-petalled or thick centered flowers such as roses, carnations, chrysanthemums and marguerites do not press satisfactorily as whole flowers but need to be broken into several parts for pressing.

When picking flowers from the garden, lay them gently in a basket as you cut them, and then dry and press them as soon as possible.

You can still find flowers to press on wet days and in the winter months by visiting a florist where you can purchase a wide range of cut flowers, foliage and potted plants.

When To Pick & Press

The optimum time to pick flowers is at midday when all the dew has evaporated. Sunny weather is best and rainy days should be avoided. If you have to pick flowers in damp weather, pick whole stems, and stand them indoors in water for a few hours until the flowerheads are dry. Pick flowers at their best, when they have just opened (and before they produce pollen), and gather some buds as well. Look out for varying sizes, unusual shapes, a variety of tints and veining, and interesting visual textures. Remember as you are pressing that you can thin out collective flowerheads such as spiraea, candytuft, wild parsley and hydrangea, so do not pass over large headed flowers.

Bought flowers also need immediate attention, so don't be tempted to enjoy their beauty for a few days before pressing, but press them while they are at their best.

Even a small courtyard garden can yield a wide range of annuals, perennials, shrubs and trees to provide flowers and foliage to press.

Equipment & Techniques

Pressed flower arranging need not be an expensive hobby: the design elements (i.e. the flowers) can cost nothing and the equipment is relatively cheap; you can even make your own press at no great expense. The amount of money you spend on a design depends largely on the cost of your setting.

Glassine photographic negative bags are ideal for storing your flowers as they are made from acid-free paper which will not attack the plant material. Aids for handling the flowers include a palette knife, tweezers and a paint brush. Miniature flowers like alyssum can be picked up with a needle point and moved about with a fine paintbrush. Larger flowers can be picked up with a palette knife or slightly dampened finger tip and then transferred to the grip of round-nosed tweezers. To fix flowers in a design use latex adhesive. Squeeze a small amount of adhesive on to a palette dish and use a toothpick to transfer a small dot of it on to the center back of a flower. Now press the flower in position.

Sprays and larger flowers may need several dots of adhesive to hold them in place, although great care must be taken to ensure that no adhesive can be seen from the front of the flower. Discard and renew the latex as soon as it starts to set in the dish.

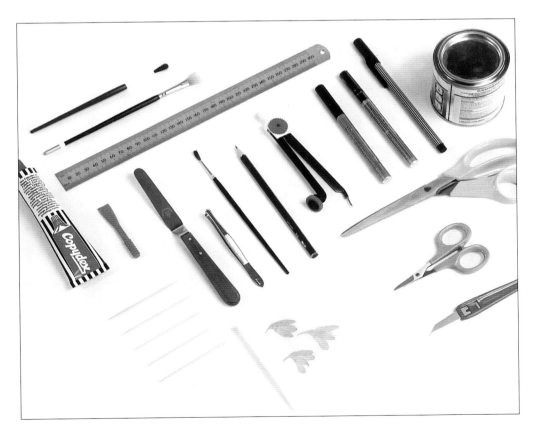

Equipment required for making pressed flower designs includes: latex adhesive and toothpicks; round-nosed tweezers and palette knife; large and small fine scissors; craft knife; ruler, pencil and compass; gold, silver and colored marker pens; assorted paintbrushes; varnish and, of course, flowers.

Making a Press

All pictures must be formed on some base; this can be paper, fabric, wood, metal or plastic, and in this book it is referred to as the design base. In choosing textiles, remember that some man-made fabrics are unsuitable in both texture and color. Old satins and silks are excellent, as are the range of velvets and fine cottons.

Art shops carry a great range of papers and boards. As a design base for pictures, parchment, marbled and watercolor papers are highly suitable. Rough textured watercolor papers and the many shades of heavyweight Ingres paper and twin-wire self-colored boards are equally suitable for making greeting cards. To make a card, first cut a rectangle of paper or board to the required size, then score (make a crease) along the fold line. Lay your card face down on a cutting board and use a blunt instrument, such as a knitting needle or the blunt edge of a scissor blade to "rule" firmly down the edge of a ruler, so making a crease in the paper. You can now easily fold along this line; if necessary trim the card after it has been folded. Before drawing on the card with a colored pen it is advisable to mark out your border first in pencil.

Large flowers can be picked up on the end of a slightly moistened finger tip before being gripped and moved about with round-nosed tweezers.

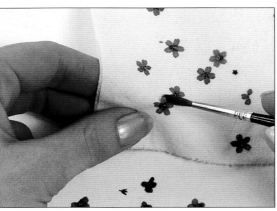

After pressing, small flowers can be removed from the tissue by bending the paper around a finger and lifting the flowers off with a paintbrush.

How to Press Flowers

1 Small flowers and leaves should be placed face down on smooth toilet tissue on top of the blotting paper. Cover them with more tissue before covering with another sheet of blotting paper. Pick sprays of small flowers and press a few whole, but snip off the individual heads of the majority and arrange in rows on the toilet tissue as shown, using a paintbrush to move them into position.

2 Larger flowers such as daffodils can be placed directly on to the blotting paper, having cut away all the harder parts with sharp scissors. Flowers pressed in profile need to be cut in half lengthwise. Put a tab sticking out from between the layers in the press to identify what flowers you have in that layer or layers, and the date when they were put in.

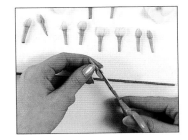

3 Multi-petalled flowers must be broken down into separate petals before pressing and should be pressed directly between blotting paper or toilet tissue. The stems, sepals (the leaf-like structures which enclose the flower) and bracts (modified leaves at the base of the flower) should be pressed separately in a press devoted to thick items. Use twice as much newspaper as usual between the layers in this press.

4 Not all leaves are suitable for pressing, and of those that are, usually only the younger ones are used. An exception is fall-colored leaves which often have part of their water content already removed naturally, due to the season. As with flowers, cut or pull the leaves from the stems and arrange neatly on the paper. If they are thick, put them in a press reserved for such material.

5 Remove all unwanted material from the blossom of trees and shrubs before pressing the flowers. Cut the backs off trumpet-shaped flowers when pressing flat, but leave the bloom whole when it is being pressed in profile. When you have finished preparing the press, put the lid on and tighten down gently. At first, tighten the press daily, then less frequently until, between six and eight weeks, the plants are dry.

Design Guidelines

Once pressed, the form of a flower loses its third dimension. So when planning a design, rather than following the guidelines of three-dimensional flower arranging, you should try to create a two-dimensional representation as in a painting.

Look at the designs on the following pages and study the color, shape and texture of each one. Then look further into the proportions, balance and rhythm of each design. Learn from the harmonizing shades and hues on page 82, the contrast of shape, color and texture on page 40, the mood of cool simplicity on page 28, the delicate miniature work on page 60, and the encapsulation of the natural beauty of the countryside on page 26. And when you have copied some of these designs, maybe you will be ready to let your personal creativity take over and become an innovator of fresh ideas.

When creating your own designs, spend time choosing your flowers and foliage, carefully considering the color and shape of each item. Consider also the size and shape of your mount or frame, and decide what shape your design is to take – the line drawings below, illustrating some basic shapes and their focal points, can be used as guidelines. Try to be confident and fix each flower straight down on to the design base rather than move it about from one place to another first – overhandling the flowers will damage their delicate structure.

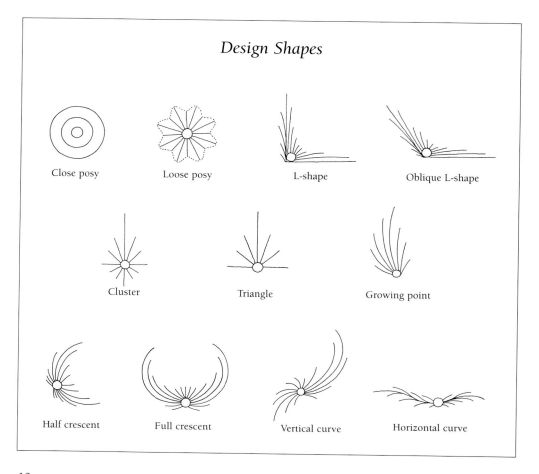

Design Shapes

Close posy   Loose posy   L-shape   Oblique L-shape

Cluster   Triangle   Growing point

Half crescent   Full crescent   Vertical curve   Horizontal curve

Mounting & Framing

Pressed flower designs should always be protected to prevent damage from handling, humidity, exposure to the atmosphere and, where possible from ultraviolet light. Humidity makes pressed flowers curl and exposure to air makes the colors oxidize and quickly fade. To avoid damage from ultraviolet light, which will also bleach colors, all designs should be kept away from direct sunlight, and as glass or acetate will also act as an ultraviolet filter, perhaps the most satisfactory protection is to have the design tightly sealed and covered by a sheet of glass or rigid plastic. As this is not practical in every application, other solutions have been found.

Sealing Techniques

Much of your early work will probably be in the form of greeting cards which require a light and flexible covering for the design. Self-adhesive, protective "library film" is available in rolls with either a gloss or matte finish. It is easy to cut, and after some practice, to smooth over the design. Practice applying library film on a few flower groups of various thickness before you attempt a finished design. Cut a generous piece of film to cover your design, then pull away one edge of the backing paper. Position the film over the design and carefully begin to rub it down with a soft cloth, gradually pulling back the backing paper as you go, and trying to avoid air bubbles. When you have finished, trim off any excess film.

Where the greeting card involves an outer card used as a "mount" for the inner design card, an acetate "window" can be fixed in position over the aperture (see below), in a way that both enhances the card and protects the pressed flower design beneath.

A slightly heavier and more durable material than library film is the "iron-on" protective film, also available in gloss and matte finishes, as well as in a "linen weave" finish which is ideal for the table mat and lampshade applications (see pages 44 and 50). It is a little more expensive than the smooth-on type, and requires some practice (and not too much heat), but it does "bond" to both flowers and base material very well and the finish gives a professional "laminated" look.

When decorating objects such as wooden boxes or glass jars, the best way to seal the design is to cover it with several coats of varnish, either matte polyurethane or one of the new ultra hard "two pack" types, depending on the base material. In these instances, the varnish can also be used to fix the flowers on to the design.

When covering an aperture in a greeting card, apply a line of "impact" adhesive around the cut-out and, while it is still wet, cover with an acetate sheet.

To cover a design with protective film, gradually pull away the backing paper and rub the film down with a soft cloth, being careful to avoid air bubbles.

Items used in mounting and framing designs include picture frames, boxes with lids designed to hold craftworks, silks and satins for the design base, ribbons and lace, design papers, acetate sheets, self adhesive "library" film, a set square, ruler and pencil, and wadding and foam sheets.

Framing Techniques

When choosing a picture frame to display pressed flower work, it is most important to make sure that the rebate in the frame (the recess which holds the glass) is deep enough to accept not only the glass, a thin mount, the design paper and the picture back, but also the wadding or foam material that is used to apply pressure to keep the flowers in contact with the glass. The picture back itself must be made of hardboard or plywood, as cardboard will not be strong enough to apply sufficient pressure. The glass must fit accurately into its frame, so that air is, to a great extent, excluded. Recommended wadding material is either synthetic wadding of the sort used in dress making, or the thin plastic foam sheeting used in upholstery. Both are equally suitable, but the depth of the rebate in the frame will decide which is best for each application.

If you have decided that your picture will be enhanced by a mount, it is advisable to prepare this before starting on your design. An artist's watercolor is often set off by a rebated mount, but in a pressed flower picture, unlike a watercolor, you must have the surface of the picture pressed

Use wadding, as employed in dress making, to pad out frames. It can easily be cut to the correct shape, and a layer pulled off if it is too thick.

To center the aperture on a mount, draw an "X" on the reverse of the mount as shown, then draw your aperture with its corners touching the diagonals.

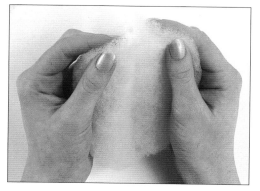

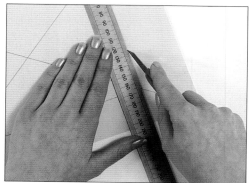

tightly against the glass. The material on which the design is to be made will have to be flexible enough to be pressed through the thickness of the mount by the wadding which must be cut to fit the aperture in the mount. So if the design material is paper or cardboard, the mount itself should be made of thin paper, and lines can be ruled on it to give an impression of depth.

The Framing Sequence

The sequence of framing a pressed flower picture depends on the material on which the flowers are being arranged. If you are using paper or board, then all the framing work can be done after the picture has been completed. However, if the material is silk or another kind of woven material, then all the backing material must be in place before work on arranging the flowers can be started.

When working with woven material, take the picture back out of the frame and clean it carefully to remove any dust or loose particles. Cut a piece of wadding and a piece of your chosen fabric just a little smaller than the back. Lay the back on your work table, center the wadding upon it, and cover with the fabric. If the picture is to have a mount around it, cut the wadding to fit the aperture. When the picture composition has been completed, use a dry paintbrush to clear away unwanted particles from the base material. Accurately position the mount, carefully lay the cleaned picture glass over it and then lower the frame itself over the glass. Slip your fingers under the picture back, keeping pressure on the frame, turn it over and place it on a soft surface. Now, while still keeping pressure on the back, use a small hammer to gently tack fine panel pins into the frame to hold the back in place. A heavy duty staple gun could be used, but be careful if using this method - if there is too much vibration some of your carefully arranged flowers could be dislodged, undoing hours of work. Finally, make use of picture tape or high-tack masking tape to seal the back and cover the nail heads. Ordinary clear cellulose tape is not suitable as the adhesive dries out; it is not waterproof, and is inclined to shrink. When using rigid rather than woven material, it is easier to pick up the finished design, lay this on top of the previously prepared wadding and picture back, and then follow the same framing procedures as described above.

When securing the picture back, keep applying local pressure while you carefully hammer in fine panel pins every 3 inches.

When the back is fully secured, use high-tack masking or picture frame tape to seal the gap. This excludes the air and covers the nail heads.

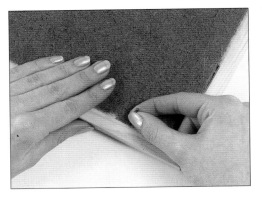

BOOKS, CARDS & TAGS

Simple pressed flower designs can turn a plain scrapbook or journal into a classy present, or be used to make imaginative greeting cards. A handmade card is a gift in itself. Framed and mounted, these delightful card designs would make charming keepsakes.

Cards can be made to suit all occasions, from Christmas to weddings and new baby celebrations. There is also an attractive array of gift tags and a bookmark which would make a lovely gift. You will find helpful advice on how to make the cards themselves (as opposed to the floral designs) in the introduction.

1 Take 17 buds of white larkspur and trim the largest one square at its base. Fix this to the book cover, about ½ inch from the bottom edge. Add a little larkspur foliage to give the appearance of a growing base. Now select the next two largest buds and fix them above the first bud.

2 Now fix larkspur buds of decreasing size, with some stems attached, in pairs up the page – one facing one way and the next the other. Make certain that the buds are all different heights. Cut a piece of matte protective film the height of the book, plus a 1 inch overlap, and the width of the design, plus ½ inch. Rub down carefully, turning in the overlap on all three sides.

Classy Scrapbook

This plain black scrapbook is enhanced by the addition of white flowers.

Candytuft Journal

This inexpensive journal is given individuality and style by the addition of pressed flowers.

1 Use *Euonymus* "Emerald 'n' Gold" leaves for the front cover. Fix them in place randomly to give a natural looking posy, adding fall-colored leaves of chervil.

2 Next, fix whole heads of pink and purple candytuft, overlapping them to create a solid effect. Finally, cut a square of matte protective library film, large enough to cover the design with a margin of about ¼ inch beyond the outermost flowers. Peel off the backing paper and rub down the film in position, taking care not to trap any air bubbles.

Valentine's Day Card

Your Valentine will appreciate this "heart full of flowers".

1 Cut a rectangle of pale blue cardboard 16 inches by 8 inches; crease and fold it in half. With a craft knife and ruler, cut out a 5 inch square from the center of the front page. Cut four pieces of lace to fit the sides of this cut-out, mitre the corners and glue in position. Fix a square of acetate to the inside of the "window".

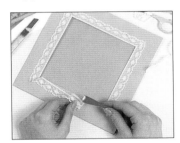

2 Also cut, crease and fold a white card to the above size. On the front page lightly mark out a "heart" in pencil, to fit within the "window", adding a few lines to break into the heart. Take a spray of *Acaena* "Blue Haze" foliage and fix to the right hand top of the heart. Add more leaves and tendrils at various points around the shape, using only pinpoint size dots of adhesive to secure each one to the card.

3 Apply a tiny dot of adhesive to the top right of the heart and, using the tip of a dry, fine paintbrush, tease an alyssum flower over it. Continue to fix tiny flowers all around the heart shape, finishing at the top with a forget-me-not. When the design is complete, carefully glue around the outside edge of the design card, and fix it centrally inside the blue card. Do not glue the back page down.

Christmas Card

This traditional Christmas card is easily made.

1 Cut a rectangle of white cardboard to measure 6½ inches by 2½ inches. Select a piece of bracken about 5½ inches in length. Fix the bracken to the card with spots of glue on the underside. Leave sufficient space at the base of this "tree" for the "flower pot". For the star, color a floret of fools' parsley gold, and glue to the top of the tree.

2 From red metallic board cut a rectangle 8½ inches by 8 inches; crease, and fold in half lengthwise. Now draw a rectangle – larger than the white card – on the red card using a gold marker. Cut out a "flower pot" from some red board, draw on some decorative lines and fix the pot to the tree. Cover the design card with protective film and fix it centrally within the gold border.

Wedding Day Card

White satin, flowers and the impression of a church steeple convey the right message.

1 Cut a piece of watercolor paper 7¾ by 11½ inches; crease and fold it in half lengthwise. Cut a triangle (base: 4½ inches, height: 6½ inches) from the front of the card, then cut a single sheet of paper to fit inside the card; pencil the triangle shape on to it.

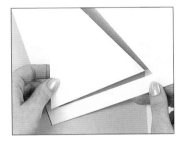

2 Cut 12 inches of ⅝ inches of white satin ribbon, fold it and stick it to the apex of the triangle, leaving a loop at the top. Trim the tails to length. Cut a further 24 inches and a 4 inch length of ribbon. Tie a bow in the long one and form bow-like loops in the short one. Sew together and glue to the top of the triangle. Fold the ribbon ends under the card and secure.

3 Take the single sheet of paper and fix rose leaves and small potentillas inside the top of the triangle. Gradually add further potentillas, gypsophilia and leaves, moving down and outward to fill the triangle. The finished look is light and spacey, giving a wedding bouquet effect. Glue a piece of acetate over the design and stick the whole sheet to the inside of the folded card.

New Baby Card

A garland of pink alyssum and blue forget-me-nots makes a delightful welcome card for a new baby

1 Cut and fold a blue (or pink) and white piece of paper to form two cards 6 inches square. Draw and cut out a 3½ inch circle from the center front of the colored card. From this circle cut out the crib and edge it as shown with lace, sticking the lace down with glue.

2 Put the white card inside the colored card, trim off any surplus paper and trace a faint pencil line through the circle on to the white card. Put the colored card to one side. Glue the crib on to the center of the white circle, then form a garland just inside the pencil line using silver southernwood leaves. Next place a cluster of pink alyssum at the quarter points.

3 Scatter a few forget-me-nots to gently break up the edge of the clusters. Cut a 4½ inch square of white tulle and fix it using latex adhesive on to the inside front cover of the colored card to cover the hole. Finally, apply glue sparingly all around the inside edge of the front cover and carefully stick the white card in position with the design showing through the window.

Thistledown Bookmark

The mass of gypsophilia floating up from the bed of pink alyssum gives the impression of thistledown on a breeze. This simple design makes an attractive marker for any book

1 Cut a strip of black cardboard 12 inches by 2 inches. Crease a line 3 inches from the top and fold under. This forms a flap to tuck over a page. Starting about ¼ inch from the base, fix clusters of pink alyssum to a depth of 1 inch. Fill in this area with leaves of thyme. From the base build up the gypsophilia, starting with the larger flower heads, and retaining some of the stems.

2 Continue up the bookmark with the gypsophilia, gradually increasing the space between the flowers. Stop just under the crease line. Now add smaller gypsophilia, taking care not to fill in too much, or the airy effect will be lost. Cut a piece of protective film larger than the book mark, and carefully rub down from the base making sure not to trap any air bubbles. Trim the film flush (so that the film fits the bookmark exactly).

Pretty Gift Tags

Turn offcuts of cardboard into pretty gift tags.

1 Cut a piece each of red metallic and glossy white cardboard 3 inches by 4 inches and fold widthwise. Secure a tip of fern to the front of the red card. Spray with gold paint and when dry, lift off the fern, leaving a red silhouette. Fix the gold fern to the front of the white card. Punch holes in the top left corners and thread with ribbon.

2 Cut a piece of single-sided glossy green cardboard 3 inches by 4 inches. Crease and fold 1½ inches from the left edge to give a folded card size of 3 inches by 2½ inches. With a green marker, draw a border inside the larger page. Fix a spray of miniature rose leaves in one corner then form a loose line of European cranberry bush flowers up the page.

3 Having looked at the construction of an envelope, make a miniature version from a 5½ inch square of paper. Glue the envelope together and line the side flaps with a silver marker. Take wispy foliage, gypsophilia and mauve lobelia and secure them inside the envelope so that they appear to be bursting out. Attach some curled mauve ribbon to the top of the tag.

4 Take some red and green single-sided cardboard and cut out some sock shapes. Using gold or silver aerosol paint, spray heads of fools' parsley; when dry, secure the best shaped florets to the heels and toes of the socks. Draw a ribbed border at the top of each sock, punch a small hole in the corner, and add colored ties.

5 Crease and fold a small piece of yellow cardboard in half and, with your compass pencil just overlapping the fold, draw a 2½ inch circle. Cut this out, leaving the card hinged together by about 1¼ inches at the top. Draw a 2 inch circle with a green marker on the front cover and fix three daisies in the middle. Refold the card and fix a length of thin green ribbon about the fold.

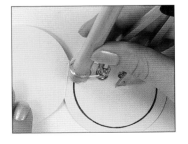

PICTURES & PLAQUES

Among the most satisfying and enduring items to make with pressed flowers are pictures and plaques. They make ideal gifts for a variety of occasions and you can never have too many of them in your home. There are a variety of different styles you can create, from the grasses and leaves used to conjure up a country walk on page 28 to the stunning oriental design on page 30. Why not make a picture to commemorate a friend or relative's special anniversary or a pretty plaque to present on Mother's Day? Details on how to mount and frame your design can be found on page 13.

1 Cut a piece of imitation parchment paper to fit a circular frame, and lightly pencil on it a 5½ inch diameter circle. Fix tips of carrot leaves around and overlapping the circle. Now add spiraea buds and erect hedgeparsley florets to fill out the circle.

2 Next take light peach-colored rose petals and fix them around and over the base of the leaves. Turn the paper in an anti-clockwise direction as each petal is secured, overlapping its neighbor, to ensure that you keep a good shape. Now secure a second row of petals over the first.

3 Take some variegated dogwood leaves and secure them in a circle, positioning the tips halfway from the top of the second row of petals. Keep moving the card around in an anti-clockwise direction as you fix the leaves. Now fix a circle of pale blue lobelia over the dogwood.

4 Fix a circle of open spiraea flowers between the first and second row of rose petals, and forget-me-not and erect hedgeparsley florets below the second row of petals. Finally, fix a ring of small rose petals within the lobelia circle and secure a cream potentilla in the center. Cut a circular mount to fit the frame, allowing space at the perimeter of the design. Frame as usual.

Victorian Posy

This type of compact posy has retained its popularity for the past century and would fit into any Victorian setting.

Country Walk

Memories of a country walk will float back when you view the mixture of grasses and leaves you have gathered and prettily arranged on a sky blue background, framed in natural wood.

1 Fresh young grass stalks, seedheads and small leaves are most suitable; make a "growing point" using ribbon, rice, and quaking grasses.

2 Having fixed the grasses down with latex adhesive, cut off the excess stems to leave a clear space in the center. Now fill this in with more grasses, trimming as you go. Finish at the bottom center with a few knapweed buds and vetch foliage, to give the impression of a "growing point". The design is framed without a mount to give a feeling of space.

Antique Miniature

Pink potentillas, highlighted against dark foliage and framed in an old gold frame, conjure up thoughts of a victorian rose garden.

1 Small, old frames can be found in bric-a-brac shops, and are easy to repair and paint. Cut a cream-colored rough surfaced parchment paper to fit the frame, and secure an irregular oval of red-tinged meadowsweet leaves. Place the largest pink potentilla centrally.

2 Fix a further six or seven mixed size potentillas with the largest at the top, interspersing them amongst the foliage to give visual depth. Make the central flower prominent by adding a few leaves under the petals. Finish by adding florets of cow parsnip to create highlights. Place the cleaned glass over the design, turn it over and put it into the frame. Put in some wadding and secure the picture back.

Eastern Inspiration

1 These double peonies should be picked when just open. Strip off the petals and bracts and press between layers of blotting paper, tightening the press daily. After five days change the paper, then tighten the press every three days until ready. Cut some heavy watercolor paper to 20½ inches by 8½ inches and arrange peony leaves in two groups as shown.

2 Next, fix bamboo leaf sprays, starting at one corner and curving them down towards the opposite corner. Intersperse some sprays between the peony leaf groups.

3 Away from the picture area, assemble the peony buds. Fix a bract on top of a small petal for the top bud, and another bract on top of two or three petals for the second bud. For the largest bud, use two bracts over four petals. Pick up the buds with tweezers and fix them in position with adhesive, tucking them under the bamboo leaves.

4 Create the smaller of the two open flowers in position over the ring of the peony leaves as follows: using medium sized peony petals, form a ring of overlapping petals around the base of the leaves. Now add a second ring of smaller petals inside the first, and complete the flower by adding wild carrot florets to the center.

5 Add a few more bamboo leaves to the large ring of peony leaves, and then use some large petals for making the irregular outer circle of the second flower. Fill in with smaller petals to make the second and third circles, and create a center with wild carrot florets. When complete, make certain that all debris is brushed from the paper before framing the picture.

Scotch Mist

The clever use of smoke tree on green velvet helps create a soft misty effect in this striking picture.

1 Remove the back from a rustic frame and cover with wadding and dark green velvet. Start the design by fixing sprays of young ash tree leaves in the shape shown.

2 Add brown beech leaves and small buds of black knapweed to fill in the outline and create a "bagpipe" shape.

3 Suggestions of the pipes are represented by seed heads of sedge. Add some spikes of heather to create a solid mass in the center.

4 Finally soften the outline by adding the wispy flowers of smoke tree around the edges of the "bagpipe". When the design is complete, take care to remove all the dust and pollen from the velvet before placing the cleaned picture glass and frame over it. Slide the frame to the edge of the table and, gripping it firmly, turn it over. Apply pressure to the back of the frame, tack on and seal.

Golden Anniversary

The charm and tranquility of bygone days are remembered with favorite flowers preserved in an old golden frame - a perfect gift for a 50th wedding anniversary.

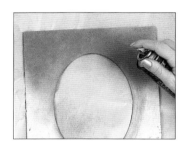

1 Old picture frames can easily be found in bric-a-brac shops and can be quickly revived with a spray of gold paint. Newer frames can be "aged" by also spraying both frame and mount with "old gold" spray paint.

2 Cut a piece of wadding the same size as the aperture in the mount, and lay it on the picture back. Cover with dark brown silk, cut to the size of the frame, and make an impression of the mount on the silk. Begin with flowers of screwstem, fixing them in the center, with the largest on top. Now add rock geranium leaves, keeping the smallest ones towards the edge.

3 Add a spray of meadowsweet to the bottom left and fill in elsewhere with individual flowers. Add a few hazel catkins for interest. Lift the edge of the largest screwstem flower with a palette knife, slip a couple of rust-colored geum flowers half under it, and add a third to its left edge for balance. Finally, soften the edges with seedheads of creeping bentgrass. Mount and frame as usual.

Mother's Day

'M' is for mother, made with flowers, and this is a gift she will always treasure.

1. Purchase a pink wall plaque from a craft shop. Take the frame, turn it over and fix some fine lace inside the rim with latex adhesive. Mark out and cut some pink cartridge paper to fit the plaque.

2. Mark out lightly in pencil a large 'M' on the pink paper. Cover the letter with stems and small leaves of salad burnet, forget-me-not buds and small grasses, securing them with tiny dots of latex adhesive. Use a curved spray of *Acaena* "Blue Haze" to create the "serifs" at the top and foot of the letter.

3. Build up over this outline with single flowers of pink, yellow and purple alyssum and slivers of pink cornflower petals. Finally, add extra foliage to balance the design and place a miniature Johnny-jump-up at the center of the 'M'. Follow the manufacturer's instructions to assemble the plaque.

BOXES & PAPERWEIGHTS

Boxes of all shapes and sizes can be decorated with pressed flowers to make that perfect gift. The designs on boxes such as the wooden one shown below need to be protected with a coat of varnish, but you can also buy an attractive range of boxes and pots from craft shops and mail order craft suppliers that have specially designed airtight lids to protect your arrangement. A selection of such pots has been used in this chapter, each incorporating an attractive floral design. A variety of glass paperweights can also be bought from craft suppliers and here you will find two imaginative ways to decorate them.

1 Begin by creating an "L"-shaped outline with leaves of Japanese maple, fall cherry, willow, wayfaring tree, hawthorn, sumach and smoke tree.

2 Continue adding the foliage, using sufficient adhesive to fix each leaf securely. Trim any overlapping pieces, so as to avoid excess bulkiness. When you are happy with the shape, coat it with a thin layer of matte varnish.

3 Now add small buds of blue lobelia, creating a sweeping curve throughout the outline. Use larger, open flowers in a cluster at the left and base of the design to form the focal point. Finish with two thin coats of varnish.

Cherrywood Box

The colors and fine grain of this beautiful cherrywood box are complemented by the subtle arrangement of fall foliage.

Little Black Box

Black forms a chic backdrop for many pale plants. Here the blue and eau-de-nil colors sit very prettily.

1 Begin by coating the lid of a small black box with special "two pack" gloss varnish. Place sprays of mugwort leaves, underside uppermost, in the left hand corners.

2 Add two mugwort sprays to the right hand corners. Now, carefully splitting a leaf spray, create a fan shape in the top center of the lid.

3 Just below the fan, in the center of the box, form a small cluster of mugwort leaves and, on top, fix a little arrangement of blue lobelia and cornflower florets. Seal the design with two thin coats of varnish.

Silk & Silver Trinket Box

The dramatic effect of white flowers against a black silk background enhances the silver plated trinket box to create a sophisticated gift.

1 These trinket boxes can be readily purchased from craft shops. Open up the lid assembly and take out the foam padding. Cut a circle of black silk to cover the padding.

2 Secure sprays of miniature variegated rose leaves in a crescent shape. Now add sprays and single flowers of gypsophilia, tucking the stems under the leaves where necessary.

3 Starting at the tips of the crescent, and building to the center, add buds and flowers of feverfew. Place a large full flower of feverfew towards the bottom center to create a focal point. When the design is complete, cover it with the plastic sheet from the lid, and assemble according to the manufacturer's instructions.

Crystal Miniature

Once you have gained confidence in using larger flowers, you will find this miniature design an exciting challenge.

1 Buy a miniature crystal bowl (available from good craft shops) and use the white card from its lid as a design card. Start by fixing the tiny foliage of shepherd's purse in place to make a full crescent outline.

2 Fill in the outline with florets of yellow and pink alyssum and elder flower. To fix the flowers in position first place a tiny spot of latex adhesive in the required place and, using a paintbrush, gently tease a flower over it, then press to secure.

3 Finally, tuck in Johnny-jump-up, keeping the largest to make a focal point towards the bottom center of the design. Place the plastic circle from the lid over the finished design, and assemble according to the manufacturer's instructions.

Christmas Boxes

This is a simple but elegant way to use empty gift boxes as containers for potpourri.

1 We have selected a green and black box. Take the lid off one of the boxes and lightly secure three whole flower heads of wild chervil diagonally across it. With aerosol spray paint, give the top of the box two light coats of gold paint.

2 When the paint is dry, remove the wild chervil to reveal the unsprayed part of the box. This shows up as a pretty pattern through the paint. Now fix the gold sprayed wild chervil to the other box lid. These boxes are filled with "Noel" potpourri, which is a festive mixture of small cones, tree bark and citrus peel. Cover the potpourri with cling plastic wrap before replacing the lids.

Fall Paperweight

Not every arrangement need be pretty and feminine. This design is perfect for any man's desk.

1 Cut a piece of cardboard to fit the recess of the paperweight and place a thin layer of latex adhesive along one edge. Fix to the strip of adhesive a selection of leaves, overlapping each other and the edge. Repeat for the other three sides then trim the leaves flush with the side of the cardboard.

2 Fill in the center of the design with smaller leaves. Shown here are hawthorn, virginia creeper, flowering cherry, spiraea, *Euonymus*, smoke tree, and *Acaena* "Copper Carpet". Overlap the foliage randomly to create a more natural appearance.

3 When the design is complete, fit it into the recess of the paperweight. If necessary, pad out with foam before sealing with the self-adhesive baize supplied.

21st Birthday Paperweight

A stunning design for that special birthday is easily created with a few flowers.

1 Begin by cutting a black card to fit the oval recess of the paperweight. Paint the figure "21" in white to the right of the oval.

2 Break up mugwort foliage and, keeping the white underside uppermost, fit it to the card following the outline of the oval. Where the foliage meets the "21", add some budded sprays of gypsophilia.

3 Intersperse a few open flowers of gypsophilia amongst the foliage then create the focal point with a large open flower of white larkspur. To complete the design, tuck a small larkspur flower under the leaves above the focal point, and place a larkspur bud below. Position the design card inside the recess of the paperweight, pad out with foam if necessary, and seal with the self-adhesive baize supplied.

DECORATIVE TABLEWARE

Flowers in one form or another always make a colorful addition to the dinner table and pressed flowers are no exception. So why not brighten up your next dinner party with one of the delightful designs featured in this chapter? There are inexpensive and easy-to-make place cards suitable for all occasions, an attractive place mat, candles and a candlestick holder. And for those prepared to spend a little more money on specialist craft items, there are also drink coasters, a tray (see right), and napkin holders, all imaginatively decorated with a beautiful range of flowers.

1 Fix a cluster of fall plumbago leaves at one end of the oval card (supplied with the tray) and at the other end fix a smaller cluster of plumbago and fall wild strawberry leaves. Now enlarge and fill out these two clusters with leaf sprays of *Acaena* "Blue Haze". Keep each cluster fairly oval in shape.

2 Working first on the smaller cluster, create a focal point with a red-tinged green hydrangea flower sitting on top of a wild carrot head. Now form a gentle curve of pink potentilla across the top of the cluster and finish off with green hydrangea and red saxifrage. For the focal point of the larger cluster place a deep red potentilla on top of a head of wild carrot.

3 To add depth, tuck some pink potentilla and red-tinged hydrangea under the carrot head. Now place two smaller red potentillas above the focal point. Make a gentle diagonal curve into the center of the design with buds of Japanese crabapple and finish off with sprays of grass. Reassemble the tray according to the manufacturer's instructions.

Afternoon tea takes on real elegance with this striking tray purchased from craft suppliers.

Tray For Two

Fuchsia Place Mat

An ingenious idea which adds individuality to any table setting.

1 Begin by cutting a rectangle of hardboard (a board material manufactured of wood fiber) 8½ inches by 11 inches. Round off the corners with sandpaper. Next, cut a piece of green marble paper to fit the hardboard. Draw two double-lined borders with green pen in opposite corners, as shown.

2 Using foliage of Ranunculus, make a triangular shape in the top left corner and an "L" shape in the bottom right. Add fuchsias to the triangle, beginning with a bud at the apex, gradually adding more open flowers and finishing at the widest part with a full flower. Repeat the process on the "L" shape, using fuchsia buds at the tips and a full flower in the center.

3 Now seal your design with a transparent linen-surface covering – the type that is ironed on. Trim the edges. Cover the back of the design card with latex adhesive and fix carefully on to the hardboard. Finally, fix a rectangle of green felt on to the reverse side of the table mat.

Carnation Coasters

These glass drink coasters - easily available from craft shops - lend themselves to a carnation display.

1 Cut a circle of moss green cartridge paper to fit into the recess of the large bottle coaster. Now fix large petals of yellow carnation, overlapping them slightly, to form an outer circle.

2 Fill in the outer circle with smaller carnation petals to create a second circle. Small petals from the center of the carnation make up the final inner circle. To complete the display fix wild chervil florets to the center.

3 Fit the design card into the recess of the bottle coaster and seal with the circle of baize supplied. Repeat this process for each drinks coaster, using different colors for an attractive display.

Chantilly Lace Place Card

This combination of cream-colored blossom and lace prettily complements traditional china at the dinner table.

1 Cut a rectangle of dark brown cardboard 4½ inches by 3¼ inches. Crease and fold it widthwise to form a "tent". Using a gold marker carefully write the desired name in the center of the top page.

2 Take about 12 inches of cream lace and, starting about three quarters of the way along the folded edge, fix it to the card with a little latex adhesive. Pinch the lace to form gathers as you round the corners and fix with a little extra adhesive.

3 Using the buds and open flowers of blackthorn, make an "L" shape at the top right corner. Use an open flower to cover the join in the lace. Create the focal point by using a pair of open flowers, glued one on top of the other. This will also give these delicate flowers greater depth. Make a similar shape, but without the focal point, at the bottom left corner.

Napkin Rings

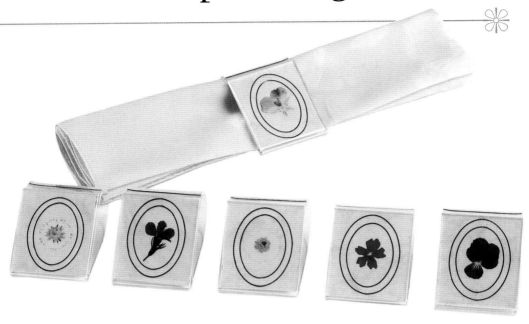

These simple but attractive napkin rings can be purchased from craft suppliers and make a perfect addition to any dinner party.

1 On a strip of green marbled cardboard, mark out an oval 2 inches by 1¼ inches with a green pen. Inside this oval, mark out a smaller one, also in green. You will need a template to achieve an accurate shape.

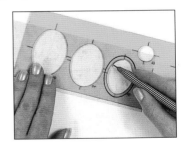

2 Repeat this procedure using a wide range of different colored flowers; used here are buttercups, blue lobelia, daisy, red verbena and different varieties of pansy.

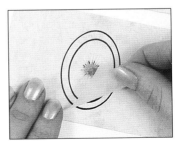

3 In the center of the ovals, fix an attractive flowerhead. Cover the design with protective film, smoothing out any air bubbles. With the aid of a steel rule and craft knife, trim the strip to fit the napkin holder.

Floral Candlestick

A plain wooden candlestick can be decorated very effectively with pressed flowers.

1 Begin by coating the candleholder with "two pack" gloss varnish. While the varnish is still sticky, adhere sprays of Ranunculus foliage to both back and front of the holder. Leave to dry.

2 Re-varnish the holder and and center a spray of montbretia buds on top of the foliage. Add larger, single buds towards the base.

3 While this second coat of varnish is still sticky, fix a cream potentilla in the center of each design. Leave the holder to dry completely before finishing with two thin coats of gloss varnish.

By Candlelight

These delicate designs transform ordinary thick candles. But be very careful not to let the candle burn down below the protective film, as the designs are not flameproof!

1 For the yellow candle, fix three fall sumach leaves in a spray with latex adhesive. Repeat twice around the candle.

2 The other candle is offset with five pink larkspur flowers fixed around the base. Rue leaves are tucked in and around the flowers. Finally, add some larkspur buds a little above the foliage. Carefully cover the designs on both candles with protective film, allowing an extra ¼ inch above the design. Rub the film down carefully and avoid trapping any air bubbles.

GIFTS & NOVELTIES

It can be great fun to break away from the more conventional types of pressed flower designs – pictures, cards, and so forth – and, instead, look around the home for more unusual objects to decorate, such as book ends, letter racks, old storage jars, notebooks, lampshades and even furniture. As this chapter shows, all these things and many, many more can be transformed with an attractive and complementary floral design and these novelties make delightful gifts.

For further gift ideas, there is a selection of attractive costume jewelry – some to be made at no great cost – and there is also a charming little perfume pot, complete with a perfume recipe.

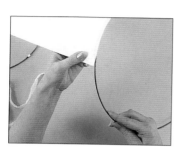

1 The unique marking and leaf formation of love-in-a-mist make an eye-catching design on a plain white lampshade. Make certain that the shade you use is of the type that has a paper or similar rigid backing to its fabric. Take it apart carefully and lay the material out to flatten. Select about eight each of small, medium and large sized love-in-a-mist flowers.

2 Spread out the material from the shade and lay the flower heads on it, with smaller flowers at the top and larger ones at the base. Make sure that no flower is at the same level as its immediate neighbors. When you have the right effect, turn the flowers over one at a time, apply latex adhesive to the center and tips of the sepals and fix down securely in position.

3 Cover the design with semi-matte, canvas textured, iron-on protective film. Cut a generous strip of film, mark the center line in pencil and roll it up from both ends towards the center. Carefully cut along the center line through backing paper only, then slowly peel off one side of backing, smoothing down the film as you go. Repeat for the other side. Iron on the film and reassemble the shade.

Lampshade

The unique marking and leaf formation of love-in-a-mist makes an eye-catching design on a plain white lampshade.

Herb Jar

Transform a "sample" coffee jar into a pretty herb or spice container. If you have several of these jars, you can make a whole series.

1 Apply a thin coat of "two pack" varnish to the front of the jar and position some carrot foliage and gypsophilia to form the outline.

2 Complete the floral design with some grass and a verbena flower. When the first coat of varnish is dry, apply a second coat over the design, feathering the edges of the varnish with a lint-free cloth.

3 Cut a circle from white sticky-back plastic to fit the top of the lid. Repeat the floral design on the plastic, fixing the plants with latex adhesive. Cover the design with protective film and fix the circle to the lid. For that finishing touch, add a band of broderie anglaise around the lid.

Perfume Pot

This solid perfume is simple to make, and looks so pretty in a matching green ceramic jar: a perfect complement to any dressing table.

1 Begin creating the floral design on the insert card supplied with the lid. Fix three variegated geranium leaves in a triangular shape using latex adhesive.

2 Follow this outline with silverweed, hop clover and two herb bennet flowers. Complete with a large herb bennet flower at the base. Reassemble the lid.

3 To make the perfume you will need 3 teaspoons of shredded beeswax, 2 teaspoons of almond oil, 15 drops of your chosen concentrated perfume oil and a drop of sap-green dye. Slowly melt the wax and almond oil over a very low heat. Remove the pan from the heat and, when the mixture has cooled a little, add the perfume and color and pour it into the trinket box. It will then set hard and be ready for use.

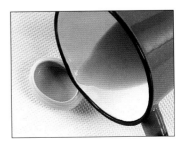

Coffee Time

Blue lobelia is an attractive addition to plain yellow enamel.

1 Start by marking out a rectangular area on the side of the pot with masking tape. Now lay the pot on its side, securing it to your work surface with an adhesive putty such as Blu-Tack. Paint the area with a thin coat of "two pack" varnish. Take care the varnish does not build up at the tape edge and form a ridge.

2 While the first coat of varnish is still sticky, position several carrot leaves to form a teardrop shape outline. When this design is completely dry, add another coat of varnish.

3 Now, fill in with the flowers. Use lobelia, beginning with buds at the top and coming down to the base with larger flowers. Fill in any gaps with foliage and add a couple of budded stems at the base to create a natural effect. When this is dry, remove the tape and give a final coat of varnish, feathering the edges by wiping them with a lint-free cloth.

Enamel Canister

This type of white enamel canister can be bought either new or second hand.

1 Secure the canister to your work surface with blobs of adhesive putty. Now take a large head of mauve candytuft and fit to the center of the canister with latex adhesive. Surround the flower with salad burnet leaves and add two more candytuft flowers on either side. Paint over the design with "two pack" varnish.

2 For the canister lid, coat with varnish before positioning a circle of salad burnet leaves – slightly apart – around the knob. Fill in between the leaves with large, single candytuft flowers. When dry, seal this design with two thin coats of varnish, feathering the edges with a lint-free cloth.

Decorative Doorplates

These specially designed door plates, available from craft suppliers, can be decorated to suit the decor of any room.

1 Cut a piece of protective film to cover the back of the plate and a piece of foam to fit the center of the plate without overlapping the holes. Then cut a rectangle of colored cardboard to fit the recess and punch holes in the corners to match those in the plate.

2 Create the design to the left with daffodils and tiny florets of cornflower. Place the design card in the recess at the back of the plate, pad out with the foam and seal the back with protective film.

3 The center design is made with sprays of montbretia buds, fall leaves and potentilla. The far left example contains specimens of meadowsweet, buttercup and cowslip.

Silver Brooch & Pendant

This exquisite piece of matching jewelry simply needs a little patience to complete.

1 Cut a white cardboard oval to fit the brooch and fix sprays of miniature maidenhair fern to create a flowing outline. Scatter gypsophilia buds amongst the foliage, then add a cluster of red alyssum in the center and blue forget-me-nots here and there. Keep the design random with tiny florets softening the outline.

2 Now cut a white oval to fit the pendant. With the aid of toothpicks, fix two sprays of shepherd's purse foliage to the top and right of the card. Arrange flower stems to resemble the stems of a bunch of flowers. Now add curving gypsophilia buds throughout the design.

3 Add buds of spiraea and shepherd's purse next, teasing them into place, over dots of adhesive, with a soft paintbrush. Use an open flower of red alyssum to form the focal point and bring some spiraea through the design from the left to the center. Assemble the jewelry according to the manufacturer's instructions.

Dressing Table Set

Plain dressing table sets such as this can be bought at good craft shops and from mail order craft suppliers.

1 Dismantle the mirror and cut some cardboard to fit. Now cut a slightly smaller piece of foam to cover the cardboard. Cover both of these with some moss green silk. Fix on to the silk three heads of wild carrot, of various sizes, to form a soft, curving outline.

2 Using white potentilla (which turns a soft creamy color when pressed) follow the outline, keeping the smaller flowers at the top and bringing the largest flower to the bottom center. Complete with a head of wild carrot to create a strong focal point.

3 Repeat a similar design on the brush using two heads of wild carrot and slightly fewer potentillas. Assemble both brush and mirror according to the manufacturer's instructions.

Scientific Classification

The following is an alphabetical list of the common names of plants used in this book and their Latin equivalent

Common name	Latin name	Common name	Latin name
Alyssum	*Alyssum*	Knapweed	*Centaurea nigra*
Apple blossom	*Malus sylvestris*	Lady's mantle	*Alchemilla alpina*
Ash	*Fraxinus excelsior*	Larkspur	*Delphinium consolida*
Bamboo	*Arundinaria*	Lobelia	*Lobelia erinus*
Beech	*Fagus sylvatica*	Love-in-a-mist	*Nigella damascena*
Blackthorn	*Prunus spinosa*	Maidenhair fern	*Adiantum pedatum*
'Blue Haze'	*Acaena*	Maple	*Acer campestre*
Bracken	*Pteridium aquilinum*	Meadowsweet	*Filipendula ulmaria*
Buttercup	*Ranunculus acris*	Medick	*Medicago falcata*
Candytuft	*Iberis umbellata*	Montbretia	*Crocosmia crocosmiiflora*
Carnation	*Dianthus carophyllus*	Mugwort	*Artemisia vulgaris*
Carrot foliage (vegetable)	*Daucus carota*	Pansy	*Viola*
Cherry blossom	*Prunus sargentii*	Peony	*Paeonia lactiflora*
Chervil	*Chaerophyllum temulentum*	Plumbago	*Plumbago capensis*
'Copper Carpet'	*Acaena*	Polyanthus	*Primula variablis*
Cornflower	*Centaurea cyanus*	Potentilla (shrubby)	*Potentilla furticosa*
Cow parsnip	*Heracleum sphondylium*	Potentilla (woody)	*Potentilla nepalensis*
Cowslip	*Primula veris*	Quaking grass	*Briza media*
Creeping bentgrass	*Agrostis stolonifera*	Ribbon grass	*Phalaris arundinacea*
Daisy	*Bellis perennis*	Rice grass	*Spartina townsendii*
Daffodil	*Narcissus*	Rose	*Rosa*
Dogwood	*Cornus alba spaethii*	Rue	*Ruta graveolens*
Elder	*Sambucus nigra*	Salad burnet	*Sanguisorba minor*
Erect Hedgeparsley	*Torilis japonica*	Saxifrage	*Saxifraxa moschata*
Euonymus	*Euonymus japonicus*	Screwstem	*Mentzelia lindleyi*
European cranberry bush	*Viburnum opulus*	Sedge	*Carex*
Fern	*Polypodium*	Shepherd's purse	*Capella bursa-pastoris*
Feverfew	*Matricaria eximia*	Silverweed	*Potentilla anserina*
Fools' parsley	*Aethusa cynapium*	Smoke tree	*Cotinus coggygria*
Forget-me-not	*Myosotis*	Southernwood	*Artemisia abrotanum*
Fuchsia	*Fuchsia magellanica*	Spiraea (spring flowering)	*Spiraea arguta*
Geranium	*Pelargonium*	Spiraea (summer flowering)	*Spiraea bumalda*
Geum	*Geum chiloense*	Sumach	*Rhus typhina*
Gypsophila	*Gypsophila*	Thyme	*Thymus serphyllum*
Hawthorn	*Crataegus monogyna*	Verbena	*Verbena hybrida*
Hazel	*Corylus avellana*	Vetch	*Vicia sativa*
Heather	*Erica*	Virginia creeper	*Parthenocissus quinquefolia*
Herb bennet	*Geum urbanum*	Wayfaring tree	*Viburnum lantana*
Hydrangea	*Hydrangea*	Wild carrot	*Daucus carota*
Japanese crab apple	*Malus floribunda*	Wild chervil	*Anthriscus sylvestris*
Japanese maple	*Acer palmatum*	Wild strawberry	*Fragaria vesca*
Johnny-jump-up	*Viola tricolor*	Willow	*Salix*

Index